T5-ACX-024

# THE PONY CRAFT BOOK

Imagine a hanger for necklaces and scarves... made from real horseshoes! Or a super cute T-shirt with a dream horse on it... one that you've made yourself! Maybe it's not that easy to imagine... But hey, it can easily be real!

Look through The PONY Craft Book and see for yourself! The book is one-of-a-kind, and it contains lots of things that every girl will like making, but especially the ones who are crazy about horses! We've written it just for you, so I hope you'll really like it.

Jannica Almblad

PS. To make some of the things in this book you'll need to use things such as an X-Acto Knife (a very sharp knife) and an iron. They can be very dangerous if you're not very, very careful. We think it would be a good idea to ask an adult for help when you need to cut or iron something.

© Helene S. Lundberg/Stabenfeldt
Concept: Jannica Almblad and Bettan Ryderheim, Stabenfeldt
Concept development, work descriptions and photography: Helene S. Lundberg
Project leader, text revisions, chapter introductions and typesetting: Jannica Almblad
Sounding board and review: Bettan Ryderheim
Proofreading: Malin Stehn
Models: Alexandra Josefsson (girl), Lady (brown horse) and Pierre (white horse)
Illustrations: Norsk Seriebyrå
Cover and layout: Brigitta Vikør, Stabenfeldt
Printed in Italy

ISBN: 1-933343-61-3

Translator: Kjell Johansson
Editor: Bobbie Chase

Stabenfeldt, Inc.
457 North Main Street
Danbury, CT 06811
www.pony.us

## STUFF FOR YOUR HORSE
– Cool saddle pad     6 - 7
– Cute noseband cover     8 - 9
– Beautiful browbands     10 - 11
– Comfy blanket     12 - 13
– Unique grooming stencils     14 - 15
– Pretty prize ribbons     16 - 19

## DESIGN PROJECTS FOR STABLE AND RIDING SCHOOL
– Pretty stable broom     20 - 21
– Cool nameplate     22 - 23
– Fun treat bucket     24 - 25
– Decorated dandy brushes     26 - 27
– Handy wall pocket     28 - 31
– Awesome jump rails     32 - 33

## HORSY THINGS FOR YOU
– Smashing scrunchie     34 - 35
– Clever stable bag     36 - 37
– Personalized riding jackets     38 - 41
– Wonderful T- shirt     42 - 43
– Spiffy stable jeans     44 - 45

## DREAM ROOM FOR THE HORSE LOVER
– Trendy desk organizer     46 - 47
– Cute bookmarks     48 - 49
– Nifty notebook     50 - 51
– Fab photo frames     52 - 53
– Loveable lampshade     54 - 55
– Posh pillow     56 - 57
– Groovy horseshoe rack     58 - 59

## FOR SPECIAL OCCASIONS
– Horsy Memory game     60 - 61
– Magnificent invitations and place cards + drinking straw decorations     62 - 63
– Pastel table setting     64 - 65
– Tasty horseshoe cake     66 - 67
– Christmas stockings     68 - 69

## PATTERNS AND TEMPLATES     70 - 80

# STUFF FOR YOUR HORSE

The horse is one of the most wonderful creatures in the world. And what can be better than getting to know a certain horse especially well, and getting really close to it? Whisper in its ear, stroke its smooth neck, smell its wonderful smell, and feel it blowing puffs of warm air against your hand.

The horse you love the most is the one you probably also want to make look the nicest. Groom it, oil its hooves, pull its mane, wipe its coat with a soft rag... And of course, having nice-looking equipment to top it all off is always good.

In this chapter you'll find examples of great saddle pads, noseband covers, browbands and fleece blankets that you can make for your horse. But the coolest things are probably the unique grooming stencil and the awesome prize ribbon.

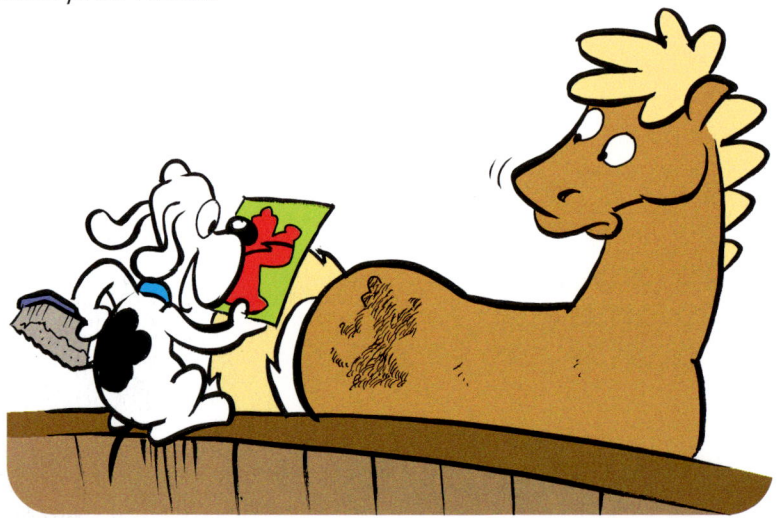

## Cool saddle pad

Are you tired of your plain saddle pad? Or maybe it's getting old and a bit worn? In that case, you can easily freshen it up with some fabric, yarn and buttons. Use a fabric that's easy to fray. Denim works well, and it's also durable and easy to keep clean. Maybe you have an old pair of jeans that don't fit anymore? Use one of the pants legs; it'll be perfect for this! Embroider letters with simple stitches, using different colors for each letter. You (or your mom) probably have some leftover buttons at home that you can use.

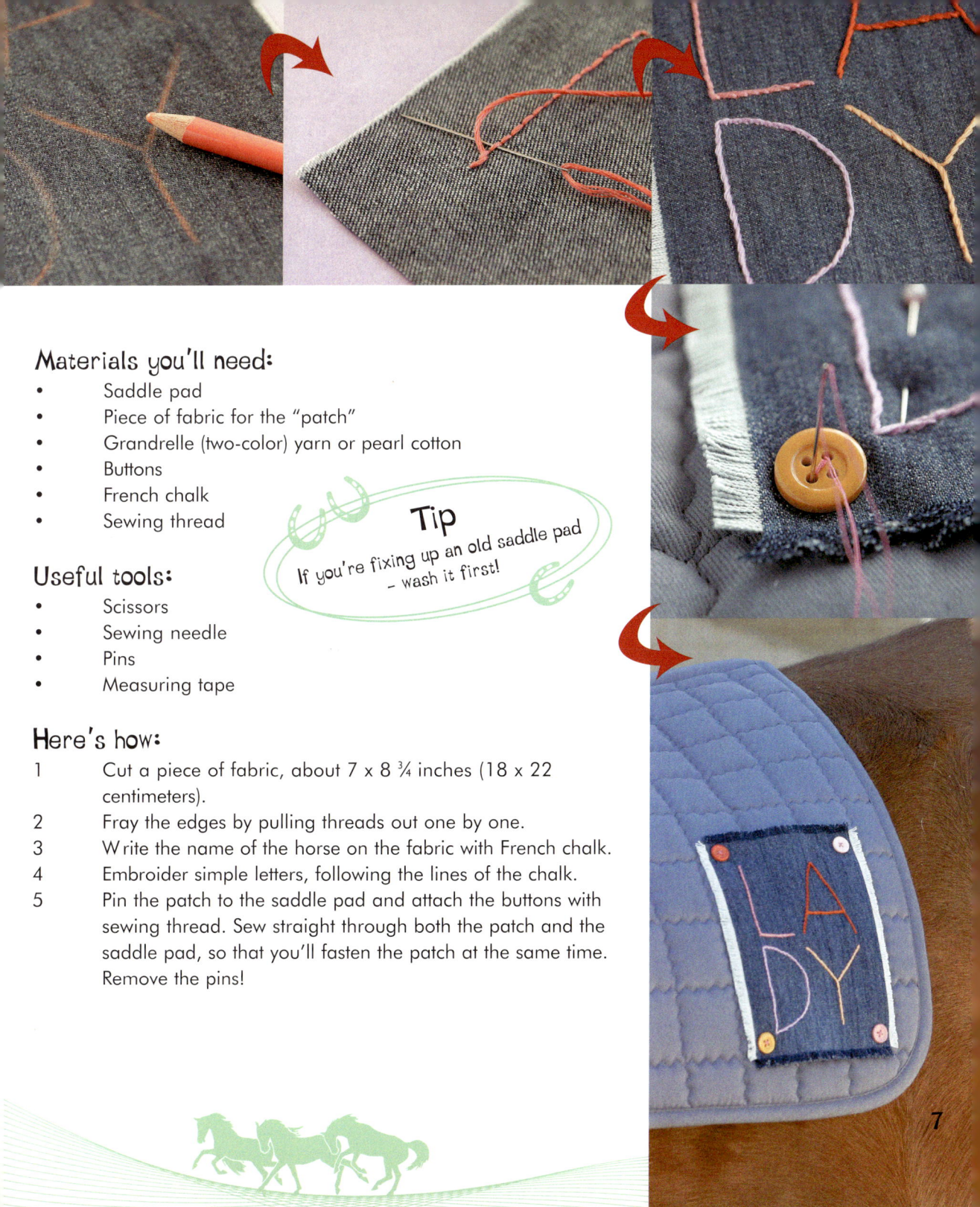

## Materials you'll need:
- Saddle pad
- Piece of fabric for the "patch"
- Grandrelle (two-color) yarn or pearl cotton
- Buttons
- French chalk
- Sewing thread

## Useful tools:
- Scissors
- Sewing needle
- Pins
- Measuring tape

### Tip
If you're fixing up an old saddle pad – wash it first!

## Here's how:
1. Cut a piece of fabric, about 7 x 8 ¾ inches (18 x 22 centimeters).
2. Fray the edges by pulling threads out one by one.
3. Write the name of the horse on the fabric with French chalk.
4. Embroider simple letters, following the lines of the chalk.
5. Pin the patch to the saddle pad and attach the buttons with sewing thread. Sew straight through both the patch and the saddle pad, so that you'll fasten the patch at the same time. Remove the pins!

# Cute noseband cover

When making a noseband cover, you have to use a soft and cozy fabric. Fleece works really well, and it doesn't fray, either. That means you can just cut the pieces without having to zigzag them. There are lots of cool, fun buttons. Mix and sew them on haphazardly and you'll have a personalized noseband cover for your horse.

## Materials you'll need:
- Fleece fabric
- Velcro
- Sewing thread
- Buttons

## Useful tools:
- Scissors
- Sewing needle
- Pins
- Sewing machine
- Measuring tape

### Tip
Use a pompom fringe instead of buttons to make a noseband cover that's perfect for Christmas. (See picture page 10.)

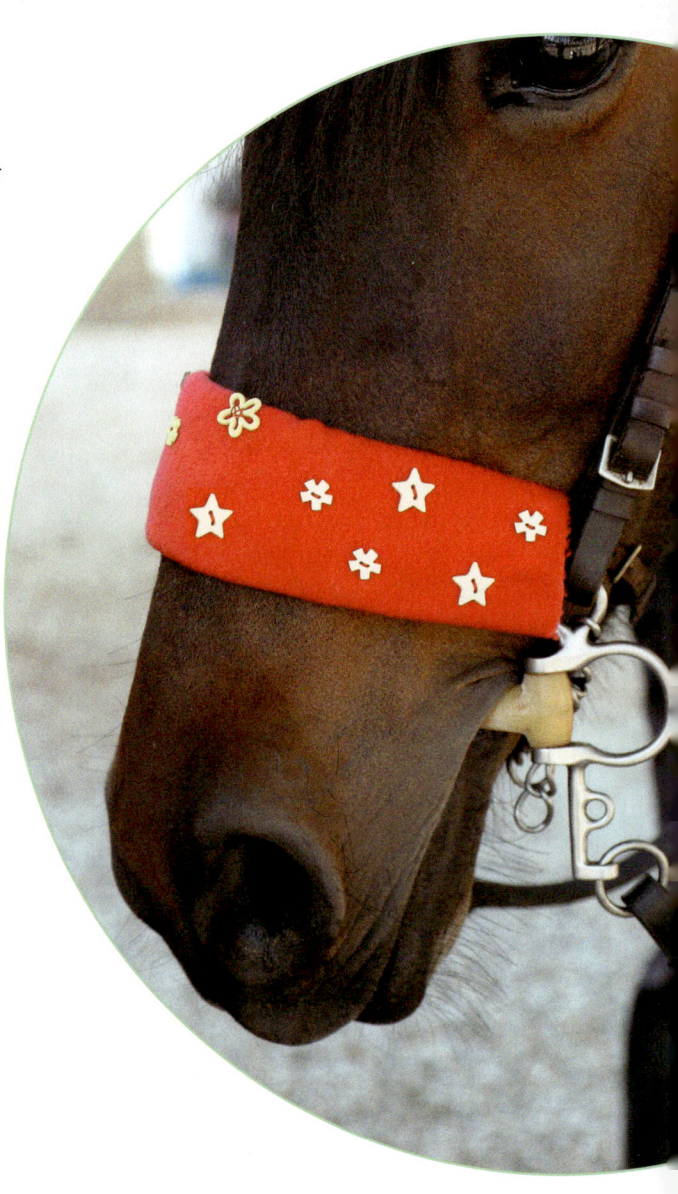

## Here's how:

1. Cut the fleece, about 6 x 11 ½ inches (15 x 29 centimeters). The size of the fabric depends on the size you want your noseband cover to be.
2. Measure the Velcro and cut 3 pieces, 1 inch (3 centimeters) each.
3. Pin the pieces of Velcro to the noseband cover. Make sure you put them on right – see picture. Try closing the Velcro before you sew it on to be on the safe side.
4. Use a sewing machine to sew the Velcro on. It's good to use a denim needle, because the Velcro can be thick to sew through.
5. Place the buttons where you want them and sew them on by hand. Stay-stitch the back to make sure they won't fall off.

# Beautiful browbands

On ordinary days you may not care that much about how the browband of your bridle looks. But for special occasions, when you want your horse to look extra-nice, it can be fun to liven it up a little. The most important thing when decorating a browband is using an appropriate glue for the materials you're using to decorate. Carefully read the label to make sure it will work. The cute pompom fringe is really for decorating pillows and curtains, for example, so you can find them at your local fabric store. The gems should have a flat back and can be bought at a crafts store.

## Materials you'll need:
- Pompom fringe
- Flat-backed rhinestones
- Glue that fits the materials and that is water-resistant (for when you wash the bridle)
- Browbands to decorate

## Useful tools:
- Scissors
- Measuring tape

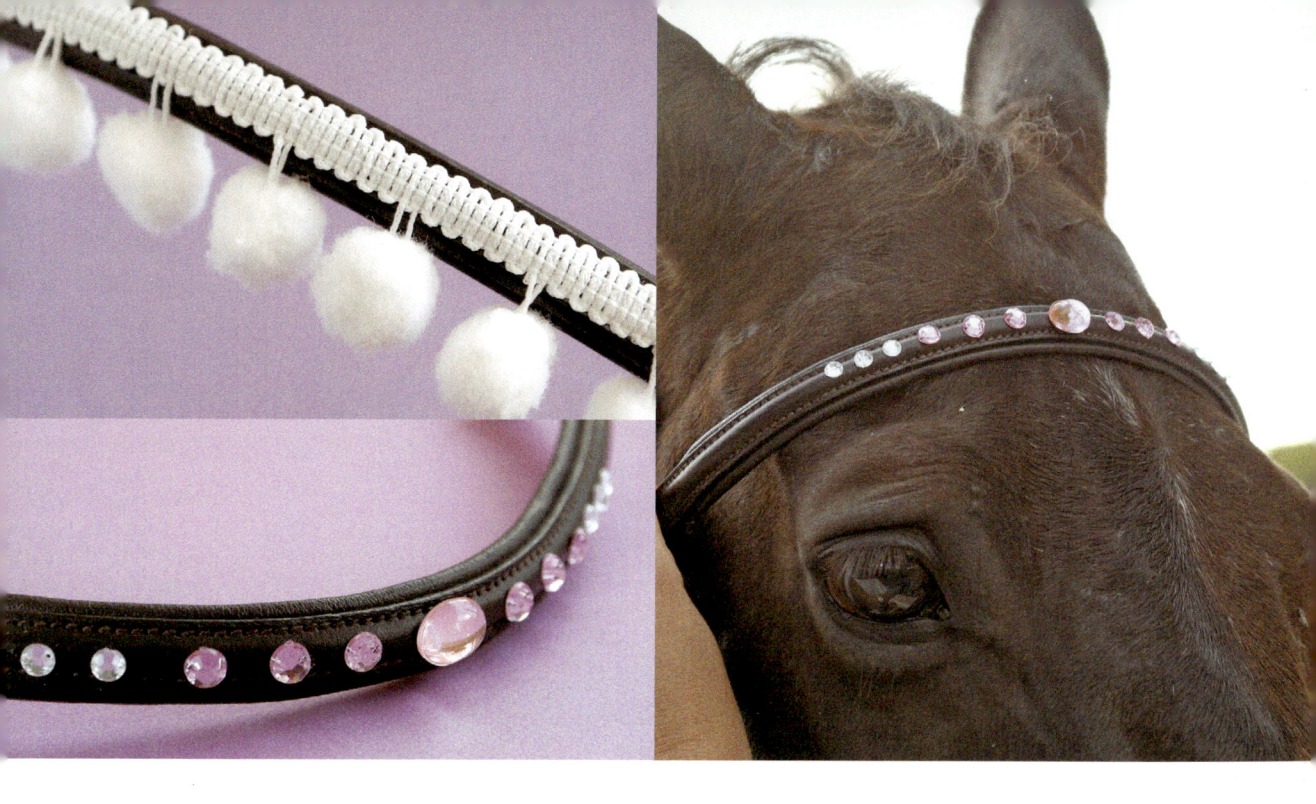

## Here's how – the pompom browband:
1. Measure the browband and cut the band with the yarn balls a little shorter.
2. Put glue on the pompom fringe – you'll need quite a lot – and put it on the browband. Press it hard to the browband, so the glue will stick.
3. Let it dry before you use it.

## Here's how – the gem browband:
1. Measure to find the middle of the browband and put some glue there. Fasten the big gem in the glue.
2. Put small dollops of glue on the rest of the browband, evenly spaced. Press the smaller stones into each dollop of glue. Do one side at a time.
3. Press all the stones firmly to the browband to make sure they're fastened properly.
4. Make sure the glue is dry before you use the browband.

### Tip
If you want to, you can combine the two styles. First glue the pompom fringe to the browband, then use the gems to decorate.

# Comfy blanket

The only seams you'll need to sew on this cozy blanket are the ones keeping the Velcro in place. You'll need a lot of fleece, depending on the size of your horse. Having a pony instead of a full-size horse will save money when making this blanket. The easiest way is to use the entire width of the fabric, and then adjust the length depending on the size of your horse. On pattern page 71 you will find a sketch of how the blanket looks. To make it stay on properly you'll need a separate girth.

## Materials you'll need:
- Fleece fabric
- Velcro
- Sewing thread

## Useful tools:
- Scissors
- Measuring tape
- Pins
- Sewing machine

**Tip**
Make a matching noseband cover in the same fabric as the blanket. The piece you cut out for the neck is enough for one.

## Here's how:
1. Measure your horse, from the middle of the neck (where the blanket should close, by the breast) to the tail. This is how much fabric you'll need.
2. Fold the fabric along the middle and cut according to the pattern; you should be cutting through both layers.
3. Cut 3 pieces of Velcro, 1 ½ inches (4 centimeters) each.
4. Pin the Velcro (at the neck of the blanket, where it should close) and check that it's put on right; try closing the blanket before you sew it on.
5. Use a sewing machine to fasten the Velcro. It's best to use a denim needle for the machine; Velcro can be thick to sew through.

# Unusual grooming stencils

Grooming stencils don't always have to be checkered. Use your imagination and create your own patterns! In a craft store or stationery shop you can find many different types of plastic. Which kind you use isn't that important, as long as it's sturdy but still easy to cut. If you use an X-Acto Knife (a very sharp knife) you'll also need a cutting mat or cutting board under the plastic while cutting, otherwise there's a big risk you'll destroy the tabletop. Ask a grownup for help if/when you need to cut.

## Materials you'll need:
- Plastic, at least Letter size (8 ½ x 11 inches)
- Pen that will write on the plastic
- Paper for a pattern

## Useful tools:
- X-Acto Knife or scissors
- Cutting mat/cutting board

### Tip
Using other patterns from the pattern pages works just as well. Many of them are good for stencils: hearts or stars, for example.

## Here's how:

1. Copy the flower pattern from the pattern pages out of paper or directly from the plastic.
2. Cut out the flower.
3. Moisten the horse's fur slightly where you want the pattern. Hold the stencil against the horse and brush against the fur.

# Pretty prize ribbons

A prize ribbon can really look any way you want it to. These are just a few examples, but you can come up with your own designs as well. There are so many nice papers and ribbons to use that it can be hard to decide what to use. The patterned paper should be slightly thinner than the circles where you write the horse's name. Double-sided tape is a great product, which will speed up your work and make it look good.

## Materials you'll need:
- Thin, sturdy paper
- Ribbon
- Glue stick
- Glitter glue
- Double-sided tape
- Pencil
- Paper for pattern

## Useful tools:
- Scissors
- X-Acto Knife
- Cutting mat/cutting board
- Ruler

## Here's how – the round ribbon:

1. Start by drawing different-sized circles. Use drinking glasses as a template to draw around. You'll need three different sizes. If the paper you want to use is too thin, you can glue it to a piece of cardboard to make it sturdy.
2. Cut notches in the medium-sized circle. You can also use pinking shears.
3. Glue the small circle to the notched circle.
4. Glue these two circles to the big one.
5. Decorate the smallest circle with glitter glue and let it dry before you continue.
6. Cut strips of thinner paper, ½ inch (1 centimeter) wide and about 12 inches (30 centimeters) long.
7. Also cut strips of patterned paper, ¾ inch (2 centimeters) wide and 6 ¾ inches (17 centimeters) long.
8. Fold the patterned strips into V shapes. Use a small piece of double-sided tape to keep them in place.
9. Put another piece of double-sided tape on the folded strip and fasten it on the back of the big circle. Put folded strips all around the circle.
10. Glue the long strips of paper on the back of the prize ribbon.
11. Cut a circle-shaped piece of paper and glue it to the back of the prize ribbon, to make that look nice as well. You can put in a paper clip, with the tip pointing upwards, before you glue the back on. It'll make an excellent suspension device.

*Make a heart-shaped prize ribbon the same way as the circle-shaped. There's a template for the heart in the pattern pages.*

Continues next page

## Tip

Vary the sizes of the prize ribbons; the one for 1st place should be the biggest, and then smaller for each place. Use your imagination and mess around with fun papers and ribbons.

19

# DESIGN PROJECTS FOR STABLE AND RIDING SCHOOL

Horses may not really care about how their surroundings look. The most important things to them are probably getting fed, getting to go out every day for some exercise, and having a comfy stall to live in.

You, however, probably like making the stable look nice. Everything that has something to do with horses is fun, right? Even sweeping the passageway can feel strangely relaxing sometimes. It's so easy to think while you're sweeping. Of course, sometimes sweeping isn't that fun.

At these times, having nice tools can help. Fix up the pitchfork and the shovel and they'll be fun, both to look at and to use! How about a broom with carrots on it, for example!?

### Tip
Paint all your tools the same color. Sweeping and cleaning out manure is extra-fun when you have colorful tools.

## Pretty stable broom

Do you want to have the coolest broom ever in your stable? Then keep reading! You'll get the best result if you use an unpainted broom. You can find good brooms at hardware stores and supermarkets. There are special paints made for outdoor use; they're hard-wearing and good, but you can use regular emulsion paint as well.

## Materials you'll need:
- A broom to paint
- Red, orange and green paint
- Black permanent marker
- Paper for a pattern

## Useful tools:
- Stencil brush
- Small pointed paintbrush

## Here's how:
1. Paint the broom. You'll probably have to paint it twice so the paint covers completely. Let it dry before you continue.
2. Trace the small carrot from the pattern pages to a piece of paper.
3. Place the template on the broom and trace the outlines. This broom has a carrot on each side of the handle.
4. Paint the carrot with orange paint and let it dry. Repeat if needed.
5. Make a few simple green lines to look like tops on the carrot.
6. Also decorate with spots, smaller on the brush itself and bigger on the handle. Use the stencil brush to make them.

21

# Cool nameplate

This is a nameplate you can screw to the door of the stall. If you put a ribbon on it, you also can take it with you when you go to a horse show. If you lacquer it when you've finished the paint, it'll look nice for a longer time. If you have access to a computer with a printer, you can easily print the name on paper and use it as a template.

## Materials you'll need:
- Oval wooden plate
- Emulsion paint in different colors
- Water-based varnish
- Carbon paper
- Ribbon
- Rhinestones and sequins
- Glue
- Ballpoint pen
- Tape
- Paper to print on

## Useful tools:
- Computer and printer
- A big and a small paint brush

## Here's how:
1. Paint the entire nameplate in the color you want the background to be.
2. Print the name from the computer. Using a fun font makes the rest of the job easy.
3. Cut the paper to make it fit the nameplate you're decorating, put the carbon paper underneath and tape it on.
4. Trace the outlines of the name with the ballpoint pen. Make sure the carbon paper is working.
5. Paint the letters on the wooden plate with a small paintbrush. Repeat until the paint covers the layer below.
6. When the paint is dry, you can use rhinestones and sequins to decorate the nameplate even more.
7. Glue a matching ribbon to the edge of the nameplate, leave the top without ribbon, and let the splice be on the bottom.

### Tip
Make another nameplate with your own name on it. You can hang it on your door at home. On the back you can write, "Doing homework – do not disturb," for example.

23

# Fun treat bucket

Fixing up a boring, ugly bucket from your stable is really easy. You just need some clear contact paper and paint. Use a paint that will work on plastic. Filling in the outlines with a black permanent marker will make it look extra nice.

## Materials you'll need:
- Bucket to paint
- Clear contact paper
- Pen that will work on plastic
- Orange paint

## Useful tools:
- Stencil brush
- Scissors/X-Acto Knife
- Cutting mat/cutting board

## Here's how:

1. Make sure the bucket is clean, otherwise there's a risk the paint won't stick like it's supposed to.
2. Trace the carrots from the pattern pages to the clear contact paper. Use a pen that will work on plastic.
3. Cut the carrot out from the contact paper. The big piece with the "carrot hole" is your stencil – meaning that's the part you'll be using.
4. Stick the stencil on the bucket. Make sure to press the edges down around the carrot shape to make sure the paint doesn't run.
5. Apply the paint through the carrot stencil using the stencil brush. You may have to do it twice if the color doesn't cover the contact paper. In that case, make sure the bottom layer is really dry before doing the next.
6. Carefully remove the contact paper and let the paint dry. Fill in the outlines with the black marker, and draw lines to make it look like a carrot.
7. If you want to, you can decorate with a matching bow, to make it look extra festive.

### Tip
Make one bucket for each thing, for example one for brushes and one for leg wraps. This makes it easier to keep all your stuff in order.

25

# Decorated dandy brushes

These brushes are decorated in two different ways. The one with the flowers is first painted white, then super-easy, colorful flowers are painted on. The other brush is made with découpage. It really looks professional, but is, in fact, very simple. Try it for yourself! For the best results, you should use wooden brushes. Write either your name or the horse's, so the brush won't get lost.

## Materials you'll need:
- Emulsion paint
- Water-based varnish
- Découpage glue
- Glitter glue
- Scraps with fun pictures
- Brushes
- Cut-out pictures for découpage

## Useful tools:
- One small and one big paint brush
- Stencil brush
- Pencil
- Scissors

## Here's how - the flower brush:

1. First, paint the entire brush white. You may have to give it two coats to make sure the paint covers completely. Let the paint dry completely before proceeding.
2. Dip the stencil brush in paint (yellow, for example) and make some circles on the brush.
3. Use the small paintbrush and make simple leaves around the circles. Press the paintbrush against the brush and pull it toward you while you release the pressure.
4. Lacquer the brush with a water-based varnish to make sure the paint won't wash off.

## Here's how - the découpage brush:

1. First, paint the entire brush white. You may have to give it two coats to make sure the paint is covering completely. Let the paint dry completely before proceeding.
2. Put découpage glue on the back of the cut-out pictures and put them on the brush. Press them on with your fingers.
3. Write either your name or the horse's name with a pencil, then fill it in with glitter glue.
4. Put two layers of découpage glue over the pictures and the entire brush. Let the first layer dry before doing the second.

## Tip

Decorate the brush with designs other than flowers. On the pattern pages, there are quite a few that you can use. If the size doesn't work, maybe you have access to a copier. That way, you can make them smaller or bigger.

27

# Handy wall pocket

Want all of your grooming equipment close at hand? Make a wall pocket, hang it on the outside of the stall door, and keep your stuff there! Use a durable and sturdy fabric, preferably cotton, which is often available in lots of nice colors. It's easy to attach the letters using vliesofix (or Wonder Under). This is a fusible webbing that you iron on. You can find it in sewing or craft shops. Use Velcro for the hangers; that way, you can easily move the wall pocket if you want to. Print the letters from a computer or draw them by hand.

## Materials you'll need:
- Durable fabrics in different colors (We used navy and red.)
- Thinner, patterned fabric
- Vliesofix (Wonder Under)
- Sewing thread
- Letters on paper
- Velcro

## Useful tools:
- Pencil
- Scissors
- Sewing machine
- Pins
- Iron
- Measuring tape

## Here's how:

1. Cut out the following pieces of fabric: backing 2 feet 8 ¼ inches (82 centimeters) wide x 3 feet 4 ¼ inches (102 centimeters) high; two pockets 12 ½ inches (32 centimeters) wide x 9 ½ inches (24 centimeters) high; three hangers 12 ½ inches (32 centimeters) long x 3 inches (8 centimeters) wide.
2. Zigzag the edges of all pieces except the hangers.
3. Fold the edges in 1 ¼ inches (3 centimeters) on the backing. Fold the corners just as you would when wrapping a gift. Sew nice running stitches using a sewing machine; it can look really nice if you use a different-colored thread and slightly larger stitches.
4. Fold the top edges of the pockets 1 ¼ inches (3 centimeters) and fasten with a parallel running stitch.
5. Cut out the letters from the paper copies, cut pieces of the same size of the vliesofix and slightly bigger of the patterned fabrics.
6. Iron the vliesofix on, but don't use the steam setting on the iron.
7. Put the letter on the vliesofix in reverse and draw along the outlines. Cut the letter out.
8. Remove the paper from the vliesofix, place the letter on the pocket and iron it on.
9. To make sure the letter won't fall off, you should also zigzag the edges using a sewing machine. It'll look nice if you use different-colored threads. Use the same method to fasten the star to the back piece.
10. Fold the edges of the pockets in about half an inch. (1.5 centimeters) If you iron them down they'll be easier to handle.
11. Place the pockets on the back piece, pin them on and fasten them with a running stitch.
12. Fold the longer sides of the hangers towards the middle so that they overlap each other (see picture) and zigzag them with the sewing machine.
13. Pin the hangers onto the back piece. Pin the Velcro on at the same time. Make sure they're on the right side of the hanger. Try closing them before you sew them on.

Continues next page

### Tip
Make a wall pocket to have in your room as well! It's great to keep all your knick-knacks in.

31

# Awesome jump rails

Jump rails are usually plain, or possibly striped. But you can easily fix up some that are much more fun, in almost no time. The jump rails hit the ground every now and then, which easily chafes the paint off. However, a stamp makes it easy to fix them up every now and then. This stamp is made from color foam, which you can find in your crafts store or your stationery shop. You glue the color foam to a piece of cardboard, and presto, you have your own stamp!

## Materials you'll need:
- Color foam
- Glue
- Paint
- Ballpoint pen
- Piece of cardboard
- Paper for the pattern

## Useful tools:
- Scissors
- Hole punch
- Flat paintbrush

## Here's how:
1. Trace the horseshoe from the pattern pages and cut it out.
2. If you're using thick color foam, cutting one horseshoe out is enough. Otherwise, you'll have to glue two together to make it thick enough.
3. Use a hole punch to make holes in one of the horseshoes.
4. Cut out a small piece of sturdy cardboard.
5. Glue the horseshoe(s) onto the cardboard. Make sure the glue's really dry before you use the stamp.
6. Coat the stamp with paint and "roll" it against the jump rail.
7. Let the paint dry before you use the jump rails.

### Tip
You can probably think of many other fun ways to decorate jump rails! Why not turn them into worms, peppermint sticks, snakes, rulers? Or paint hearts, stars, spots, apples, carrots...!

33

# HORSY THINGS FOR YOU

Riding apparel has a tendency to become quite dirty and worn pretty quickly, but you still usually want to look nice when you go to the stable.

You can't really keep buying new clothes all the time. After all, the clothes are usually more comfortable when they've been used for a while.

Of course, you can always pep up your clothes a little. That old plain jacket, for example - if you wash it and sew on an appliqué, it'll suddenly be fun to wear again. Or your old jeans - decorate them with patches of a nice fabric, and they'll be like new again! Well, almost, at least.

## Smashing scrunchie

Having your hair look good on important days is a must. Turn a regular scrunchie into a festive, luxurious hair decoration. Thin organza ribbons work well for this. Since they're so thin they won't collapse. Mix the colors however you want – the more colors the better. And of course, if you have long hair you have to have a ponytail when you're at the stable!

## Materials you'll need:
- Scrunchie (hair elastic)
- Organza ribbon in lots of different colors

## Useful tools:
- Scissors
- Measuring tape

## Here's how:
1. Cut the ribbons to about the same length – 10 inches (25 centimeters) is good.
2. Put the ribbons around the scrunchie and tie them together.
3. Repeat around the entire scrunchie until it's filled with the ribbons.

### Tip
If the ribbons fray, you can just even them out with scissors.

# Clever stable bag

Of course your horse should have its own treat bag. Use a durable fabric that's easy to wash if you put carrots directly in the bag. The appliqué is much easier than it looks. Use vliesofix (fusible webbing); you can buy it at your sewing/craft shop.

## Materials you'll need:
- Sturdy fabric for the bag
- Decoration fabric
- Sewing thread in different colors
- Vliesofix (Wonder Under)
- Cord
- Paper for pattern
- Pencil

## Useful tools:
- Scissors
- Sewing machine
- Iron
- Pins
- Safety pin
- Measuring tape

## Here's how:
1. Cut the bag out in one piece, 21 ¾ inches (55 centimeters) high x 19 inches (48 centimeters) wide.
2. Zigzag the edges of the entire piece.
3. Trace the carrots from the pattern pages on paper and cut them out.
4. Iron vliesofix to the back of the decoration fabric and draw around the outlines of the edges of the carrot pattern. Cut the "carrots" out.
5. Remove the paper from the vliesofix and iron the carrots to the front of the bag.
6. Decorate by zigzagging; use little lines to make it look more like carrots, with green tops sticking out from the carrots.
7. Fold the fabric along the middle, right side in. Sew the bottom and side together, but leave the top 3 inches (8 centimeters) open.
8. Fold in the seams and sew a slit, see picture.
9. Fold the upper edge down 1 ½ inches (4 centimeters) and sew a casing 1 ¼ inches (3 centimeters) down.
10. Cut a piece of the cord, about 28 inches (70 centimeters), and run it through the casing, using a safety pin at one end.
11. Tie the ends together, fill the bag with carrots and hurry off to the stable!

## Tip

If you make a handle you can easily hang the bag on the handlebar on your bike. Cut a piece of a thick ribbon and sew it on the back of the bag. If you thought this bag was fun to make you can sew one for your gym clothes as well. Maybe the appliqué on that one will be a pair of sneakers?

37

# Personalized riding jackets

Do you have a plain riding jacket that's starting to feel a bit boring? Decorate it just the way you want; here's some stuff to inspire you! Are you a glamour girl or do you prefer letters as decoration? Print the letters from the computer – that way you can decide the style you want them to be in. It's easy to fasten the decorations with vliesofix, which is a fusible webbing that you iron on. If you prefer the horseshoes in gold and silver, you should iron some thick vlieseline (a fusible webbing like vliesofix, but it is single-sided, with glue on one side, whereas vliesofix is double-sided) before sewing them on with a sewing machine, using a small zigzag. Decorate with nice rhinestones that you sew on by hand.

## Materials you'll need:
- Jacket
- Decoration fabric
- Vliesofix
- Vlieseline
- Sewing thread
- Paper for pattern
- Rhinestones
- Pencil

## Useful tools:
- Scissors
- Sewing machine
- Iron
- Sewing needle
- Pins (Straight pins)

## Here's how
### - the jacket with the letter:

1. Print a letter from the computer or draw your own on paper. Cut it out.
2. Iron vliesofix to the back of the fabric, a piece that's as big as the letter.
3. Put the letter, reversed, on the vliesofix and draw along the outlines. Cut it out.
4. Pull off the paper from the vliesofix and iron the letter to the jacket. Put cotton fabric between the jacket and the iron if the jacket's made from a synthetic material.
5. Thread the sewing machine with different color thread. Sew along the edges of the letter with a small zigzag.

39

Here's how
- the "glamour jacket":

1. Draw two horseshoes (pattern page 74) on regular paper. Cut them out.
2. Iron thick vlieseline to the back of the gold/silver fabric.
3. Trace the horseshoes on the fabric and cut them out.
4. Pin them on the back of the jacket and sew them on with a small zigzag.
5. Sew some matching rhinestones on the horseshoes. Sew them on by hand and make sure to fasten the threads carefully on the inside of the jacket.

### Tip
Decorate the front of the jacket as well. Make the patterns a little smaller, so they fit on a pocket, for example.

41

# Wonderful T-shirt

It's really fun to decorate your own T-shirt, and you can make it look just the way you want it to. On the pattern pages, you'll find a horse that's a good size for a regular T-shirt. It's painted with a glittery fabric paint and the outlines are filled in with a relief liner. The ends of the tail, the mane and the neckline have tiny little pink rhinestones that you actually iron on. You'll find all the materials at your crafts store.

## Materials you'll need:
- T-shirt to decorate
- Paper for pattern
- Glittery fabric paint
- Relief liner for fabric
- Iron-on rhinestones
- Invisible fabric pen (Pen for use on fabric that becomes invisible after a few hours)
- Thick cardboard to put inside the shirt for protection

## Useful tools:
- Paintbrush
- Pencil
- Scissors
- Iron

### Tip
Buy the materials with a friend and make the shirts together. There's paint for more than one shirt, and it'll be fun to have a "friend shirt."

## Here's how:

1. Trace the horse pattern from pattern page 80 and cut it out.
2. Put a piece of thick cardboard between the layers of fabric of the shirt so the paint won't bleed through.
3. Place the horse on the shirt, making sure that the cardboard is placed underneath, and draw the outlines of the horse with a trick marker pen.
4. Trace the outlines with a relief liner for fabric. Let it dry completely before you continue. Read on the package how long this will take.
5. Paint the horse with the blue glittery fabric paint. Its mane and tail get to be gold-glittery. Let this, too, dry before you continue.
6. Remove the cardboard and put the shirt on your ironing board. Put the iron-on rhinestones in place and iron them on; read the instructions on the package.

43

# Spiffy stable jeans

With a nice decorative fabric your old jeans will be "like new," and at least ready to wear in the stable. Use a fabric that can be washed in the same way you wash your jeans.

## Materials you'll need:
- Jeans
- Decorative fabric
- Vliesofix (fusible webbing)

## Useful tools:
- Scissors
- Iron

## Here's how:
1. Iron the vliesofix to the back of the decorative fabric and cut the shape out.
2. Remove the paper from the vliesofix and place the decoration where you want it on your jeans. Iron it on.
3. If you want to, you can zigzag the edges of the decoration or sew simple stitches around the edges.

### Tip
If the jeans are too short you can use the decorative fabric to lengthen them.

45

# DREAM ROOM FOR THE HORSE LOVER

*No matter how much you want to, you can't bring your horse back with you to your room. That's one friend who's going to have to stay at the stable.*

*But there are some things you can do to not forget him or her. (OK, there's not much chance of that, but still!) You can decorate your entire room so it'll be obvious to everyone that someone who loves horses lives there. And you can do it with pictures of your favorite horse. In this chapter there are seven horsey things you can make. The desk organizer and the bookmarks match really well, but the horseshoe rack is probably the coolest thing.*

## Trendy desk organizer

You need at least one desk organizer on your desk. And regular cans really can look awesome with the help of some paper. Make sure to save the cans before they go in the trash. Also make sure they're really clean before you start decorating them. There are lots of different nice papers; use these along with matching ribbons. Of course, there has to be a horse on it, as well.

## Materials you'll need:
- Aluminum or tin cans
- Patterned paper
- Satin ribbon
- Horse picture
- Plain paper
- Double-sided tape
- Thick double-sided tape
- Glue
- Pencil

## Useful tools:
- Scissors
- Measuring tape
- Ruler

**Tip**
Make more desk organizers and give them away to your stable mates.

## Here's how:
1. Measure the circumference and height of your can. Cut a piece of the same size of the patterned paper.
2. Put double-sided tape along the top and bottom of the paper, put it on the can and press it on with your fingers.
3. Cut out a horse picture and tape it onto a plain piece of paper. Cut a frame a little less than half an inch (1 centimeter) around the picture.
4. Put the photo with the "frame" on the middle of the can; use thick double-sided tape.
5. Cut a satin ribbon as long as the circumference of the can.
6. Put double-sided tape on the inside of the ribbon, and put in on the edge of the can. Press it on with your fingers.

# Cute bookmarks

For all your PONY books, bookmarks can be useful. You can find loads of patterned and plain papers at your crafts store or stationery store. Make bookmarks from these and decorate them with nice horse pictures and satin ribbons. You can either use pictures of your favorite horses or scraps and stickers.

## Materials you'll need:
- Paper in different colors and patterns
- Glue stick
- Ribbon
- Horse pictures

## Useful tools:
- Scissors or X-Acto (cutter)
- Cutting mat/cutting board
- Hole punch
- Ruler

# Here's how:

1. Cut two pieces of paper, one plain, 2 ½ x 7 inches (6 x 18 centimeters), and one patterned, 1 ½ x 7 inches (3.5 x 18 centimeters).
2. Glue the smaller piece on in the middle of the bigger; use a glue stick. Press it on with your fingers. It's a good idea to press it under some books until it's really dry.
3. Decorate the bookmark with a horse picture that you glue on as well.
4. Make a hole with the hole punch half an inch (1 centimeter) from the bottom at the middle of the bookmark.
5. Cut 2 pieces of ribbon, 13 ½ inches (34 centimeters) each.
6. Put the ribbons together and fold them at the middle. Pull them through the hole in the bookmark and pull the ends through the hoop. Tighten.

## Tip
This is a perfect gift for other horse fanatics, and will definitely be appreciated. While you're at it, you might as well make a few.

49

# Nifty notebook

Turn an ordinary notebook into the coolest ever! Use a photo of your favorite horse and frame it nicely on the book. Then decorate the notebook with the horse's name, rhinestones... Your imagination is your only limit!

## Materials you'll need:
- Notebook
- Paper to cover the notebook with
- Photo
- Paper to put the picture on
- Letter stamps
- Stamp pad
- Double-sided tape
- Glue

## Useful tools:
- Scissors or X-Acto (cutter)
- Cutting mat/cutting board

## Here's how:
1. Cut the paper you're going to cover the book with. It should be the same size as the front, back and spine added together.
2. Put double-sided tape along the spine and edges of the notebook and put the paper on top. Press it on with your fingers.
3. Cut a piece of paper in another color, about one quarter inch (0.5 centimeters) bigger than the photo.
4. Tape the photo to the middle of the paper, which then becomes the frame.
5. Tape the photo with the "frame" on the notebook and press it down carefully.
6. Stamp or write the horse's name underneath the picture.
7. Decorate the notebook with a cool gem that you glue on right below the name.

## Tip
Do the same with binders and other things you have on your desk.

51

# Fab photo frames

Photo frames shaped like horseshoes aren't things you see every day – and yet, they're so simple to make! There are lots of nice papers to choose from. You'll find all the necessary materials in a crafts store/stationery shop. Write the horse's name with a matching pen and hang your frames in matching satin ribbons.

## Materials you'll need:
- Sturdy paper
- Flat-backed rhinestones
- Horse pictures
- Glue
- Double-sided tape
- Thick double-sided tape
- Satin ribbons
- Paper for pattern
- Pen

## Useful tools:
- Scissors or X-Acto (cutter)
- Cutting mat/cutting board
- Ruler
- Hole punch

## Here's how:

1. Trace the horseshoe and the nameplate from pattern page 74 to a piece of paper and cut it out.
2. Draw the part on the nicer paper using the other template on page 74 and cut it out.
3. Also, cut a square to put the horse picture on, slightly larger than your picture. Fasten the horse picture on the squares with double-sided tape.
4. Make holes at the top of the horseshoe with the hole punch.
5. Glue the rhinestones on. Let the glue dry before you continue.
6. Put two pieces of thick double-sided tape on the "nameplate" after writing the horse's name on it. Remove the backing and put it on the horseshoe.
7. Put the horse photo on the back or front of the horseshoe.
8. Hang your frame with a nice satin ribbon. Tie a bow at the top.

### Tip
Make the frame, but skip the holes at the top. It'll look really nice glued to a binder or notebook.

53

# Loveable lampshade

Fix up your lampshade – it's really fun, and it'll look great when it's finished! You can use a picture of your favorite horse, or some other appropriate picture. If you have access to a color printer you can print a picture to use. Decorate around the picture with colorful sequins. You can find all the materials at your local crafts store.

## Materials you'll need:
- Lampshade
- Horse picture
- Découpage glue
- Pen
- Sequins
- Wide paintbrush
- Pencil

## Useful tools:
- Scissors

## Here's how:

1. Start by choosing an appropriate picture. Cut it into a circle, or keep the picture as it is.
2. Place the picture on the lampshade and draw around the outline softly with a pencil.
3. Remove the picture again and apply découpage glue about one quarter inch (3 millimeters) outside the drawn line.
4. Place the picture on the glue and use the paintbrush to press it on. At the same time, put a layer of glue on top of the picture.
5. Let it dry and then add one more layer of glue.
6. Before the glue is dry, put the sequins in the glue right outside the picture.

## Tip

If you want the lampshade to be another color, you can paint it before you decorate it. Use regular water-based emulsion paint. Let it dry before you start decorating the lampshade.

55

# Posh pillow

Having lots of pillows on your bed is really cozy – especially if they have horse images, of course. This pillowcase is made from linen and the edges have been frayed, and it's decorated with a paper napkin. It's both easy to make and looks great – your mother will probably want a pillow of her own!

## Materials you'll need:
- Linen or other fabric that will fray
- Pillow
- White textile paint
- Napkin with horse image
- Relief liner
- Sewing machine
- Découpage glue

## Useful tools:
- Sewing machine
- Scissors
- Straight pins
- Flat paintbrush
- Measuring tape

## Here's how:
1. Cut two pieces of the fabric the same size; about 3 ¼ inches (8 centimeters) bigger than the pillow.
2. Measure and mark with pins on the fabric where you're painting the background square. Paint it with white fabric paint and repeat if needed. Make sure the paint is really dry before you continue. Fix the paint according to the instructions on the package.
3. Cut the horse image from the napkin and carefully remove the white layers; you only need to use the top layer.
4. Measure the horse image and apply découpage glue on a corresponding part of the white square.
5. Carefully place the napkin in the glue and lightly apply another layer of découpage glue on top of it. Let it dry, and then apply another layer on top. Again, let it dry.
6. Decorate the edge of the napkin horse with a relief liner. Let it dry.
7. Put the parts of the pillowcase right side out and pin them together.
8. Sew the pieces together with a wide, tight zigzag. Leave an opening so you can put the pillow in.
9. Put in the pillow and sew the opening closed. It's easier if you first sew large stitches by hand (tack) before using the sewing machine.
10. Fray the edges as much as you want to.

## Tip

If you don't want the frayed edges, cut the pieces of fabric about ¾ inch (2 centimeters) bigger than the pillow and then sew it right side in. Turn it right-side-out and put the pillow in, then sew the opening together by hand.

57

# Groovy horseshoe rack

Your own rack with a real horseshoe is as cool as it is useful. The only thing you need is a piece of wood, some paint, screws, screw nuts and a horseshoe. You can find the silhouette of the horse and rider on pattern page 76. Adjust the size of the silhouette to the size of the wood you're using. You can easily make it bigger or smaller using a copy machine. Ask a grownup for help when you're going to drill the holes. You can probably get some help cutting the wood at the hardware store.

## Materials you'll need:
- Piece of wood, about 16 x 10 inches (40 x 15 centimeters)
- Paint for the wood
- Paint for the silhouette
- Wood screws
- Screw nuts (to create space)
- Horseshoe
- Paper for a pattern
- Ballpoint pen
- Carbon paper
- Black permanent marker
- Tape

## Useful tools:
- Screwdriver
- Scissors
- Flat paintbrush
- Small paintbrush

## Here's how:

1. Paint the board the desired color. Repeat until the paint covers the wood completely.
2. Trace the horse silhouette from the pattern pages to a white piece of paper.
3. Put the paper on the board with the carbon paper in between, and trace the edges with a ballpoint pen.
4. Remove the paper and fill in the outlines with a black permanent marker.
5. Paint the silhouette, with a black color, for example. Repeat until it's covered and let it dry.
6. Mark the holes of the horseshoe where you're going to screw it to the board.
7. Put the screw in the horseshoe and put 2-3 screw nuts on the screw. They should be bigger than the screw, so you can slip them on, not screw them on. Do the same in the other hole.
8. Screw the horseshoe to the board.

## Tip
If you need more hooks you just need to use more horseshoes and a longer board.

59

# FOR SPECIAL OCCASIONS

If you like horses, it can be really fun to have a horse-themed party, for example for your birthday. Invitations, table settings, even the cake, can be horsey. If it's possible you can have your party outside or at the stable. That way even the horses can join in!

But if that isn't possible, maybe Star and the others will have to wait for Christmas. As the saying goes, "Good things come to those who wait."

### Tip
Use a digital camera and print the pictures from your computer. It can also be fun to mix the pictures of horses with photos of other animals, your friends and your family.

## Horsey Memory game

Playing Memory with pictures that you know on the cards is much more fun than a regular game with random pictures. The deck is super-easy to make, and it's even easier if you use a steel ruler and an X-Acto (cutter). Be careful with your fingers – you can get seriously hurt if you slip with the X-Acto. When you send in non-digital film for development it usually isn't that expensive to make extra copies. For the back of the cards you should use a small-patterned paper; otherwise the cards won't look the same and you'll be able to recognize them easily. You decide for yourself how many cards you want. Make as many as you feel like – the more there are, the more difficult the game.

## Materials you'll need:
- 14-ply (1 mm thick) poster board
- Horse pictures (two of each)
- Paper for the background, for example small-patterned wrapping paper
- Spray glue

## Useful tools:
- Scissors
- X-Acto knife (cutter)
- Cutting mat/cutting board
- Steel ruler

## Here's how:
1. Glue the patterned paper to the poster board using spray glue. Remember to be somewhere where it doesn't matter if you spill when using the spray glue; being outdoors is a good idea. Open the window if you're gluing indoors!
2. Put a clean white paper on top and smooth it down with your hands. Remove the top paper and let the glue dry.
3. Cut your pictures so they're all the same size. 2 ½ x 2 ½ inches (6 x 6 centimeters) is a good size.
4. Glue the pictures on in the same way as the paper and smooth them down with your hands.
5. Cut the cards out using an X-Acto knife (cutter), a steel ruler and a cutting mat/cutting board. Let the glue dry.
6. Let the games begin!

# Magnificent invitations and place cards + drinking straw decorations

A successful party starts with fancy invitations that you give to your friends. Then you only have to match the place cards and the rest of the decorations. It's fun to see how surprised your friends are when they view the results. Choose paper in colors that you think will fit the theme. Sometimes you'll be surprised by how well two colors work together, even though you never thought they would. Glitter glue is a great thing to use to decorate cards and more; it'll be even more festive if you embellish it with a gold pen. Unleash your imagination!

## Materials you'll need:
- Paper in two different colors
- Horse pictures
- Double-sided tape
- Glitter glue
- Gold pen
- Drinking straws
- Thick double-sided tape or glue
- Pen
- Paper for a template

## Useful tools:
- Scissors or X-Acto (cutter)
- Cutting mat/cutting board
- Ruler

## Here's how - the invitations:

1. You're the one to decide how big you want the cards, but it's smart to adjust them to the envelopes you're sending them in. For example, split letter paper in two and fold the pieces at the middle. That'll make two invitations.
2. Cut a window on the front of the card.
3. On the inside, at the same height, put a horse picture with double-sided tape.
4. Cut out a heart. There are a few to choose from on the pattern pages. Write the invitations on the heart and glue it below the horse picture.
5. Decorate the window corners with glitter glue or gold pen.

*Let the party begin!*

## Here's how - the place cards:
1. You can get about 5 place cards from one piece of letter paper. Cut them out and fold along the middle.
2. Tape on a horse picture, write the name of the horse or the rider, and decorate with glitter glue in the corners.

## Here's how - the drinking straw decorations:
1. Trace a horse silhouette from the pattern pages; there are two different sizes to choose from. Cut it out.
2. Decorate the horse with gold pen and glitter glue.
3. Measure how high the glasses are, so the horse won't get wet. Then tape the horse to the drinking straw or glue it on with regular glue.

# Pastel table setting

There's so much fun stuff to do when you're going to have a party with your (stable) friends. Here's an example of place cards and napkin rings. These are pastel colors, but of course yours can be whichever colors you want. There are many nice things you can use to decorate them, for example tiny ready-made bows or hearts that clip onto the paper. You'll find lots of fun materials at a crafts store or stationery shop.

## Materials you'll need:
- Paper (semi-thick)
- Satin bows
- Metal hearts to clip on
- Pencil
- Paper for template
- Glue

## Useful tools:
- Scissors or X-Acto knife (cutter)
- Cutting mat/cutting board
- Ruler
- Hole punch

## Here's how - the place cards:

1. Trace the horse silhouette from the pattern pages to a regular paper and cut it out.
2. Fold a colored paper along the middle and place the template so that the tail and stand are right at the fold. Draw around the edges lightly with a pencil.
3. Cut the horse out in double paper.
4. Glue the bow on with a small dollop of glue.
5. Write the guest's name in the middle of the horse.

## Here's how - the napkin rings:

1. Trace the two parts of the napkin ring from the pattern pages and tape them together to make a whole.
2. Draw the pattern on the colored paper and cut it out.
3. Carefully cut the slits open.
4. Make a hole with the hole punch at each end of the horseshoe. Also, make a small hole in one side and attach the heart.

### Tip
Let your friends bring their place cards and napkin rings home - as a fun party favor.

# Tasty horseshoe cake

This cake isn't as difficult as it looks. Take your time and be as careful as possible, and it'll turn out great! Remember to never mash and mix kiwi and cream; the cream will curdle. Decorate your cake with any edible fruits and berries you can get hold of. If you want to, you can use canned fruits.

## Ingredients for the cake:
- 3 eggs
- 1 cup of granulated sugar
- 4 tablespoons (½ stick) butter
- ½ cup of water
- 1 ½ cups flour
- 1 ½ teaspoons of baking powder
- 1 teaspoon vanilla extract

## Other ingredients:
- Whipped cream
- Powdered sugar
- Vanilla pudding
  (Buying a mix is the easiest)
- Strawberry jam
- Strawberries
- Kiwi fruits
- Oven paper (aluminum foil)

## Useful tools:
- 350-degree oven
- Large bowl
- Knife
- Cake pan
- Ring mold pan
- Spatula
- Hand-held electric mixer
- Saucepan

### Tip
Make the cake with your friends once the party's started – baking's really fun!

## Here's how:

1. Whip eggs, granulated sugar and vanilla extract on high speed with a hand-held electric mixer; the batter should be fluffy.
2. Melt the butter in a saucepan, add the water and let it come to a boil.
3. Whip the butter/water mix into the egg batter and keep whipping it hard.
4. Mix all the dry ingredients and sift them into the batter. Stir as little and as carefully as possible.
5. Pour the batter into a greased baking pan.
6. Bake at the bottom of the oven for about 40 minutes. Check with a cake tester that it's done before you take it out.
7. Leave it in the pan for a while before you tip it onto a wire rack to let it cool.
8. Cut the cake as in the pictures.
9. Mix the custard according to the instructions on the package. Spread it over the first layer of cake.
10. Put on the next layer of the cake and spread the strawberry jam over it. Put on the last layer of the cake.
11. Whip the cream hard and add some powdered sugar while you're whipping it; 1 tablespoon for 1 ¼ cups of cream is usually good.
12. Spread the cream carefully over the entire cake. Wipe off any spillings from the plate, to make sure it'll look nice.
13. Cut the rinsed fruit and decorate the cake however you want.
14. Dig into your super-tasty cake!

# Christmas stockings

Surprise your stable mates by making a Christmas stocking for each of them. Putting a small gift in each is enough – it's the thought that counts. Sew a little hanger on each stocking; that way you can hang it wherever you like. Decorate the stockings however you want. We used white felt, which is easy to sew onto the stockings, and which doesn't need to be zigzag stitched. One stocking got icicles and the other a heart with a button on it. These stockings are quite small, but if you want them bigger you just have to change the size of the pattern.

## Materials you'll need:
- Red fabric
- White felt
- Two-color (Grandrelle) yarn or pearl cotton
- Button
- Pen
- Red ribbon for hanger
- Sewing thread

## Useful tools:
- Scissors
- Sewing machine
- Straight pins
- Sewing needle
- Measuring tape

## Here's how:

1. Trace the stocking, the icicles and the heart from pattern pages 77 and 73 on a piece of paper. Cut them out.
2. Put the stocking pattern on a folded fabric with the right side in, pin it on and cut about half an inch (1 centimeter) outside the edges. Lengthen the stocking about 2 inches (5-6 centimeters) at the top. Cut it out.
3. Pin the icicle and heart patterns to the felt and cut them out.
4. Pin and sew the heart to one of the stocking parts with simple stitches, using grandrelle (two-color) yarn or pearl cotton. Sew the button on with regular sewing thread.
5. Put the stocking parts with the right side in, pin them together and sew them together with a running stitch, using a sewing machine.
6. If you want to be extra careful, you can zigzag the edges of the stockings. This will reduce the risk of the fabric fraying and keep the stockings nice for years.
7. Cut a piece of ribbon for a hanger, about 6 inches (15 centimeters). Pin it to the top edge of the stocking.
8. Fold the top of the stocking down and pin it there. On the stocking with the heart, sew the edge with big stitches in white grandrelle yarn or pearl cotton.
9. Pin and sew the icicles and ribbon on with big stitches in red grandrelle yarn or pearl cotton.

## Tip

If you don't have access to a sewing machine you can make the stockings entirely out of felt. Place the pieces right-side out and sew them together around the edges with small, simple stitches. That'll look great too.

# Patterns and templates

On the following pages you'll find lots of nice patterns and templates that you can use to make the things in this book. Of course, you can always make your own patterns/templates as well; just unleash your imagination!

If you need to enlarge a pattern – and don't have access to a copier – you can do it using a grid.

## Here's how:

1. Draw a frame around the entire picture. Use a pencil and a ruler. The frame should preferably be whole inches/centimeters both ways (for example, 4 x 5 inches or 10 x 12 centimeters rather than 3.94 x 4.72 inches or 10.7 x 12.3 centimeters).

2. Mark every inch or centimeter along the frames, both the sides, and top/bottom. (If the frame's 10 x 12 centimeters, that means 9 marks each along 2 of the sides and 11 each along the others.)

3. Make long lines between the short – horizontally and vertically – until the entire frame is filled with a grid. The squares should be ½ X ½ inch or 1 x 1 centimeters. Write numbers above the grid, starting with 1; write letters to the left of the grid, starting with A.

4. Take a paper that's big enough and draw a twice-as-big (or more, depending on how big you want the new pattern) frame on it. (If your small frame is 4 x 6 inches, and you want the pattern twice the original size, that means the new frame should be 8 x 12 inches.)

5. Do just what you did during the second step, but mark every 1-inch or 2 centimeters instead.

6. Make long lines between the short, both horizontally and vertically. In this grid the squares should be 1 x 1 inches or 2 x 2 centimeters.

7. The hardest part is still left – to fill in the 1 x 1 inch or 2 x 2-centimeter squares! Look at each ½ X ½ inch or 1x1-centimeter square and draw what you see in the corresponding 1 x 1 inch or 2 x 2-centimeter square – but twice as big! When you've filled in every 1 x 1 inch or 2 x 2-centimeter square, your enlargement is done.

71

73

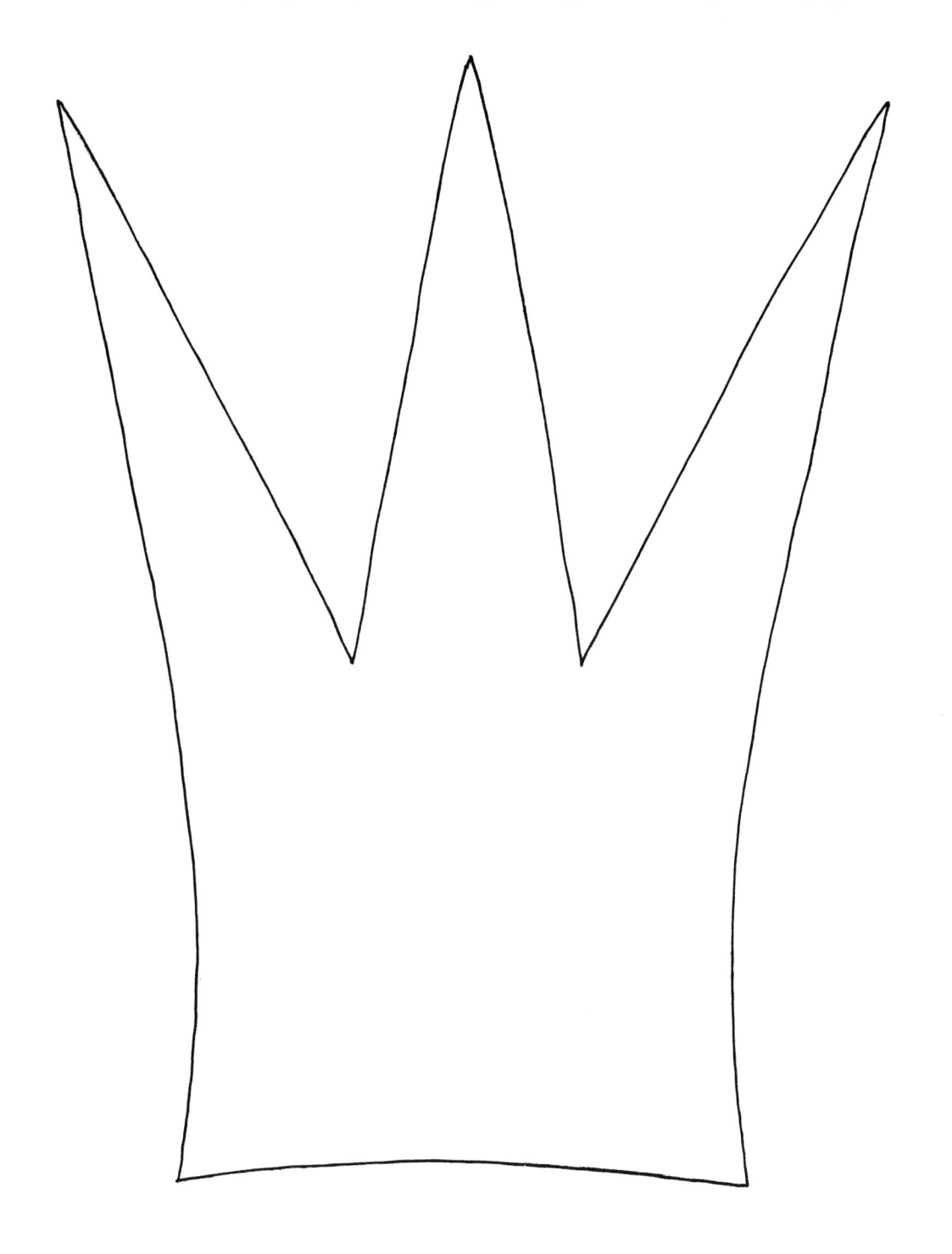

74

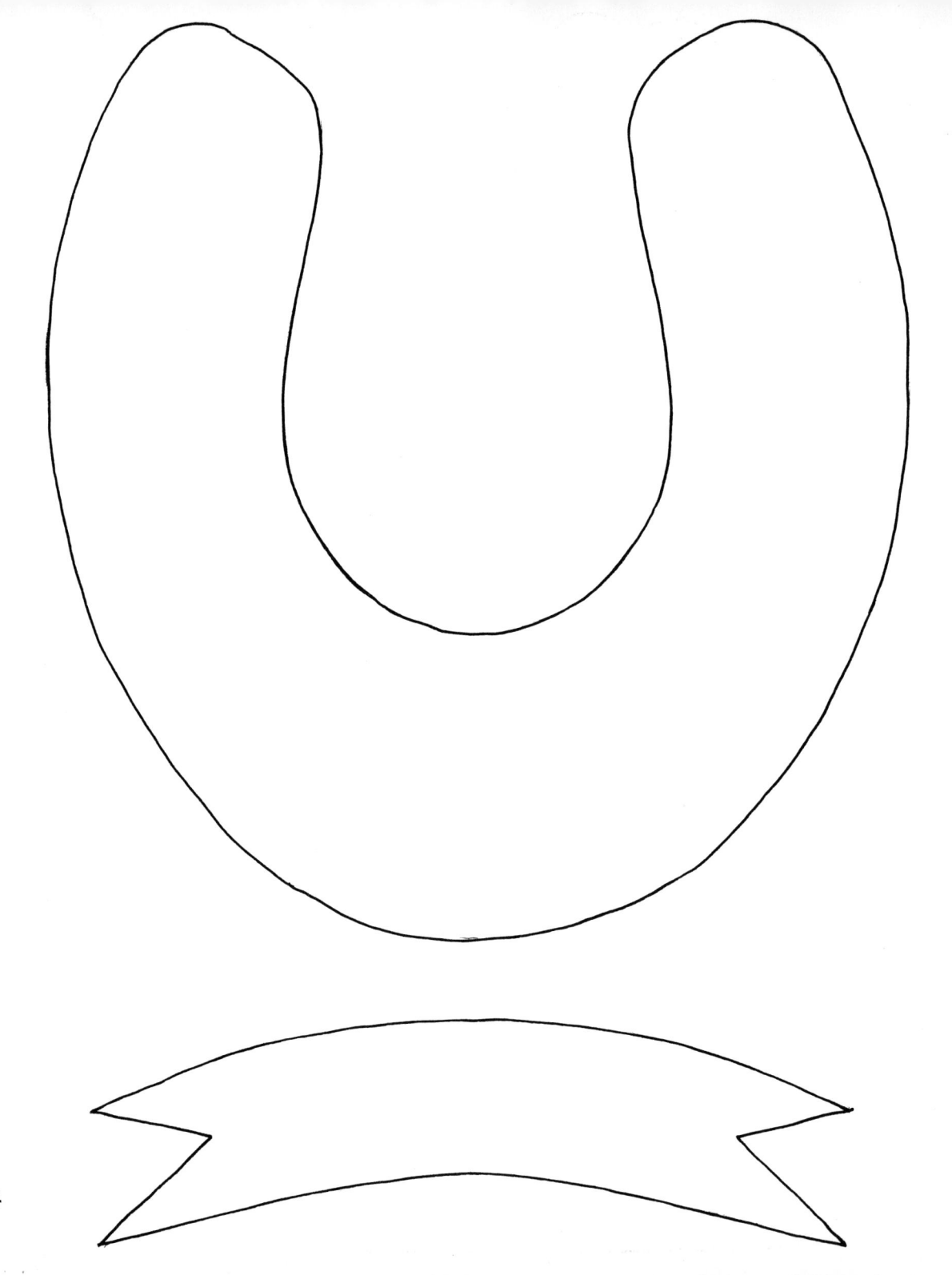

75

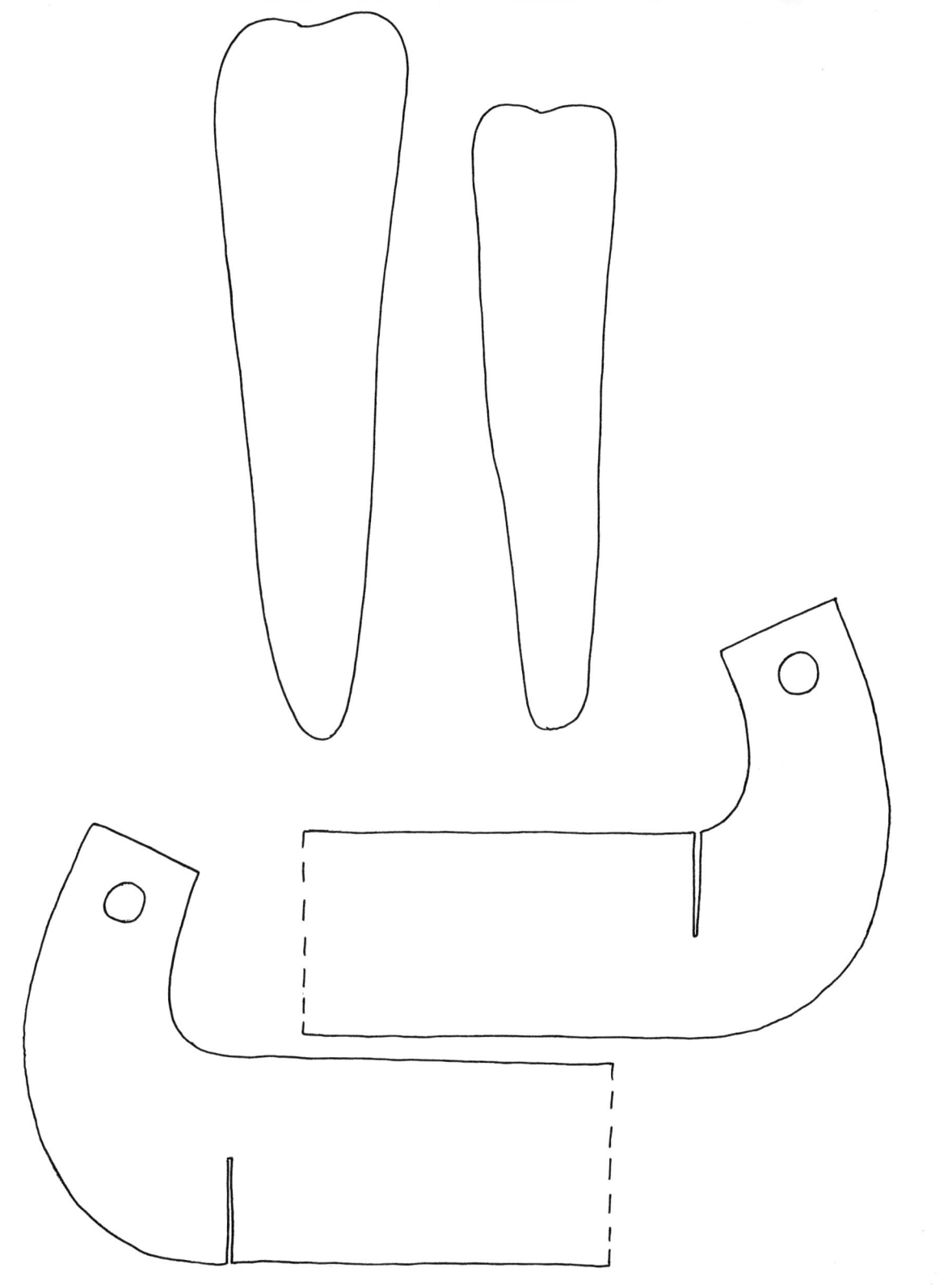

78